Leo Hartley Grindon

The Little Things of Nature

considered especially in relation to the divine benevolence

Leo Hartley Grindon

The Little Things of Nature
considered especially in relation to the divine benevolence

ISBN/EAN: 9783337023836

Printed in Europe, USA, Canada, Australia, Japan

Cover: Foto ©ninafisch / pixelio.de

More available books at www.hansebooks.com

THE
LITTLE THINGS OF NATURE

CONSIDERED ESPECIALLY IN RELATION TO THE

DIVINE BENEVOLENCE.

BY

LEO HARTLEY GRINDON,

AUTHOR OF "LIFE, ITS NATURE, VARIETIES, AND PHENOMENA," "PHENOMENA OF PLANT LIFE," ETC.

SECOND EDITION, REVISED.

BOSTON:
T. H. CARTER AND SON.
1866.

Stereotyped and Printed by
ROCKWELL AND ROLLINS,
122 Washington Street, Boston.

PREFACE

TO THE
SECOND LONDON EDITION.

THE following Papers make no claim to a scientific character. They are little more than brief notices of a few of the phenomena of nature, given in a way that the least experienced may understand.

The rapid sale of the first edition of this work, and the favor shown by the public towards "Life, its Nature, Varieties, and Phenomena," and to the "British and Garden Botany," have been sources of great satisfaction to me.

85, RUMFORD STREET, MANCHESTER.

The Vitality of Seeds.

AMONG the most wonderful things in Nature are to be reckoned the Eggs of Birds and of other creatures, and the Seeds of Plants. An atom, often not so large as a grain of sand, and apparently endowed with no greater amount of living energy, expands, almost while we watch, into a lively animal; or it unfolds a green point, which, nourished by the rain and sunshine, becomes the architect of a charming flower or a noble tree. Did we not behold the miracle repeated incessantly before our eyes, it would be difficult to believe that life could be so concentrated; but, like all other grand truths, it comes before us so much as a matter of course, that we are apt to overlook its marvellousness, bestowing our highest and foremost admiration upon the brilliant and the sonorous,—the lightning, the awful roll of the cloud-born thunder, or the beautiful upward-streaming glory of the Aurora. No doubt these are things that deserve our deep and most reverent interest, alike on account of their incomparable grandeur as natural phenomena, and of their fine significance as emblems of realities in the inner, invisible world. We should, however, accustom ourselves to consider, with an equal delight, the common every-day occurrences by which nature is sustained, and upon which we depend for our personal and daily comfort.

It is a great mistake to suppose, that to find the most striking illustrations of the Divine Love and Wisdom in the arrangements of the visible creation, we are necessitated to look at what is immense and magnificent. Just as the happiness of life does not depend upon the half-dozen memorable enjoyments that make certain years and days stand out in the annals of our past, like the green and palmy islands of the desert to the traveller, but upon the small and unconsidered blessings that come fresh and fresh every hour and every moment; so does a truly intelligent idea of the munificence, the skill, the taste,—if such terms may be used,—also of the far-reaching providence that anticipates every want before it can possibly be felt, and of the ease and the infinite power of Him who holds the heavens in his hands, come less of the consideration of mighty phenomena that happen rarely, and rather as exceptions, than of the daily observation of that quiet and pretty ripple of life through the tiny and tender forms of bee and butterfly, flower and fern, and feathered moss, which imparts a kind of immortality to the scenery amid which we tread, and makes us cry out, with old Isaac Walton, as he listened to the song of the nightingale, "O Lord! if these be thy gifts to thy creatures upon earth, what hast thou not prepared for thy saints in heaven!"

The preservation of the vital spark in Seeds, and its sudden burst into vegetable fire when kindled under the laws that at once protect and call it forth, is exemplified as well as we could desire in the most ordinary operations of horticulture. When the parent plant decays, those little germs in which, with a loving farewell, it wraps up its best energies, along with incredible capacity for bright color, and sweet smell, and grateful taste, are collected by the gardener, carefully dried, and put away; every seed, he well knows, is a storehouse of sleeping life, which, with the return of Spring, if placed where rain and sunshine can pay alternate visits, will leap into green infancy of fair blossom or wholesome vegetable. Nothing more is wanted to prove the *fact;* but over and above this ordinary, familiar proof, there is a class of occurrences less known than they deserve to be, which are calculated to excite our wonder to the utmost. Properly-ripened seeds, if placed in certain conditions, are literally *immortal.* That is to say, they are capable of retaining their growing power indefinitely; not merely for a few years, not merely for a few centuries, but for thousands of years, — how long, indeed, no man can say. The earthy crust of our planet appears to be stocked in every part with seeds that have been produced in years gone by, scattered upon the surface, and subsequently covered up with soil. Whenever the ground is disturbed, either by the plough, or by the spade of the railway excavator, or for any purpose which causes its depths to be overturned, — that portion which was many feet below being thrown to the surface, and exposed to the air, the sunbeams, and the moisture of dew and rain, — immediately there springs up a crop of young plants, certainly not originating in seeds only just then brought from neighboring fields, and, as certainly, from seeds that have been lying in the soil for ages. How they came to be covered up is easy to conceive, when we see with our own eyes what is done by wintry floods, and the sweeping down of great masses of earth and soil, which accumulate often to a considerable depth, and are no doubt similarly charged with seeds, which, after waiting their turn, will some day grow. For it is a clearly established fact that no seed can germinate or begin to sprout, unless it have the threefold influence in direct operation upon it, of warmth, moisture, and the atmosphere. Let it be shut in from the access of these, and it lies passive, giving no sign of life or growth, and incapable of doing so.

How wonderful to think that this crust of the earth upon which we daily walk so thoughtlessly, is at once the cemetery of five or six thousand billions of men and women, so far as regards their terrestrial bodies, they themselves being all vigorously alive in another state, — and a storehouse of the germs of innumerable plants and flowers! What a provision in it for the perpetual renewal of the earth's green carpet! Let blight, or locusts, or the cold grip of an inexorable frost, change it to brown barrenness, the simple upheaval of a few feet of soil would soon furnish material for clothing it anew. God never leaves himself without a witness. The world is never so drowned but some little ark swims upon the water's top with a treasury of new blessedness; and could we conceive it possible that desolation should afflict the earth's surface, under the laws of natural calamity, we are assured that from the granaries below there would soon flow an abundant restoration.

Some persons have tried to refer this wonderful circumstance of the immediate growth of plants upon newly turned-up soil to an origin inconsistently called " spontaneous generation," that is to say, development out of earth, sand, and water, and any other odds and ends of inanimate matter which might happen to be collected together. No doubt, if it pleased the Almighty to sow life afresh upon our planet, he could do so. It may be in conformity with the laws of his Divine Order so to do. But all that it has been permitted to man to learn and think in reference to this subject, is opposed to the idea of plants and animals ever now arising except from seeds and eggs produced by previous individuals or pairs of the same species. We are never justified in going to *super*natural causes for the explanation of occurrences which a calm and reverent exploration will show to have their rise in *natural* causes; and no ground has ever yet been shown for supposing that the plants which appear on railway embankments and any similar places, cannot have originated in the way described.

True, there is a great deal that is very perplexing in regard to the apparently spontaneous development of *some* forms of living things, such as of grubs in flour and bran. But the perplexity is the sign merely of our ignorance of particulars that no doubt it will be granted to future generations of men to discover. It is certainly no proof that the hypothesis of spontaneous development is a reasonable one. We are under no circumstances justified in trying to accommodate facts that we do not understand to speculations that are not founded upon other and well-established facts. If they will not fit, our wisdom is to wait. No one can discern the seeds in the earth; yet they are there. So are the germs in the bran, waiting, like the former, for their needful stimuli. Nothing is ever got by arguing from our ignorance; nor is anything ever got by too much eagerness and haste to possess it. "Tarry ye the Lord's leisure," is a principle wise to observe alike in method of life and in philosophy. If materialists, who look with approval on such hypotheses as that of "spontaneous development," would first seek to learn all that it has pleased God to disclose concerning development according to the laws of order, as exhibited in the regular succession of plants and animals, and in the history of the human heart and mind, they would find that no philosophy is so wise and good, and will help them through so many difficulties, as that which starts from the spiritual and from MAN; and primarily from the Divine Humanity, which — with all reverence be it spoken — is the point from which run the avenues to all science and all nature, and in which they all converge, like the branches of a tree in its pillar-stem.

Special examples of the growth of long-buried seeds upon newly turned-up soil are easy to cite. Some of the most extraordinary are those where poppies are the subject. No plant in nature is more remarkable than the poppy. Humble in its growth, its juice is one of the most powerful sedatives known to medicine, while the essence of that juice, called *morphia*, is one of the most powerful of vegetable poisons. At night the flowers close in a peculiarly elegant manner, — sleeping as if lulled by their own lethean balm; the petals, instead of being laid smooth and flat in the bud, as happens with almost every other flower, are squeezed and crumpled together, so that they never become perfectly straight; and when they expand, they do so with such force as to thrust off the green chalice that encircled them as a cradle. Every capsule, or "poppy-head," contains hundreds of minute seeds, which are beautifully chased upon the outside, so as to form exquisite objects for the microscope, without which the embossing cannot be seen; and lastly, these seeds, when they fall upon the ground, seem indestructible. They only spring up, however, and form new poppy-plants when the earth which contained them is lightly disturbed. Trodden in, so that the earth is compacted, and elbow-room, as it were, denied to them, they lie without any effort to grow. Of course, under such circumstances, they cannot be stimulated by the threefold essentials, sunshine, air, and moisture. There is little doubt that within these last few years, and probably this very last summer, crops of the wild crimson poppy of our own country have sprung up from seeds which were ripened at that remote period in the history of the fragment of Europe we now call Britain, when no portion of it was occupied by human beings. The geological character of the surface and subjacent layers shows that thousands of years must have rolled away since the parents of these poppies flaunted their gay apparel in the sunshine; and but for the accidental disruption of the soil that contained them, they would apparently have retained their growing power for ages to come.

When tracts of forest-land are cleared of the timber, as often happens in North America, and occasionally in our own country, the following season there springs up in abundance where the trees stood previously, some pretty herbaceous plant that was quite unknown there while the trees existed, and which had been patiently "biding its time." The explanation of such curious appearances is perfectly simple. The herbaceous plant, whatever it may be, had occupied the ground when there were no trees there, forming some kind of herbage or meadow, and letting fall its annual progeny of seeds. In course of time trees have sprung up, their own seeds conveyed thither either by human agency, or by one or other of the wonderful contrivances of nature which insure propagation, whether man give his aid or not. These trees have offered too dense a shade for the herbaceous plant, which retires, as it were, into private life; but when they in their turn are cut down, the original plants return, covering the surface with the old imperishable carpet. Is the mortality or the immortality of nature the more wonderful? Every season the ranks of the vegetable population of our planet are smitten by death,—there seems no hope for their restoration. There is no sound, no movement, to show that life is still throbbing; yet, with the first kisses of the new-born year, the necropolis changes into a scene of nimble and beautiful growth, and we see that it was not destruction that was effected by the cold touch of winter,—that nothing had really perished; but that it was life that had retired awhile to gather itself up for a new effort,—simulating death,—and which now bursts forth again in all the old exuberance and sprightly sweetness. What looks like death in nature is never anything more than the highest and essential part of its life, pausing awhile that it may start anew. The forms in which it is clothed are cast away; but the life never gives way for a single instant.

And this is the grand lesson to be learned from the consideration of seeds, and their wonderful vitality. Every particular seed contains within itself the life of the plant, just as one's own true life resides in the spiritual body. Our leaves and blossoms drop away with autumn; the white snow descends upon our brows, its flakes tremble in the wind; the colors fade; the force declines; presently the whole of the poor, old, worn-out frame sinks helplessly in the dust, never to rise again; but who or what is *dead?* Cross the dark river, which in the material world is represented by winter, and then all that is worth having is found safe, and shining in the sweet lineaments of renewed youth!

Many kinds of seeds are gifted with powers not merely of retaining life under the ordinary circumstances of nature, but of resisting the most terrible attacks. When wine has been made from raisins, and the refuse has been scattered over the fields as manure, it has been observed that the grape-seeds have vegetated, and produced young vines; and this notwithstanding the boiling and fermentation they have had to endure. The seeds of elder-berries have been observed to grow after similar trials. Many experiments have been made to ascertain exactly what amount of unnatural heat seeds can bear without being destroyed. It considerably exceeds that which plants can bear; and the same is the case with respect to extreme cold.

Thus are the wonderful phenomena of nature not only good and delightful to contemplate in themselves, but intrusted with the higher value of representing the great truths of religion. There is probably no true doctrine in matters of religion which is not somewhere illustrated in the processes of nature; certainly there is nothing in the benevolence of God with regard to man for which we may not find some exquisite parallel among the forms of humble nature, learning from them even to understand it better, because shown in so simple a way. The "diligent hand" always "maketh rich," both in worldly possessions and in the best of all knowledge, which is that of the Love and Wisdom of God.

The Sleep of Plants.

WALKING through the decorated fields of Summer, before the scythe of the mower has laid their sweet crowds low, or along the paths of some well-trimmed garden, rich with the floral spoils of many distant lands, and noting the cups and chalices of their thousand blossoms, as they drink the tender warmth of the sunshine, we naturally imagine that the condition of a flower, whether wild in the country, or forming part of the elegant and cultivated company of the parterre, is to remain, after once expanded, like the Electric Telegraph Office, "open always." Our ideas rest, as in all other matters, upon what we happen to behold at the moment, and this partial truth is believed to be the whole; and this temporary condition—for it really is no more—to be the prolonged and the abiding one; the abiding one, that is to say, until the flower shall have worn out its little lease of life, and petal and stamen, calyx and honey-bag, alike dissolve and are lost in the bosom of mother earth, from which all things come, and to which all return.

Flowers, ordinarily, are *not* "open always;" those of many of the largest and most important classes of plants close as regularly as day changes to night, remaining shut during the hours of darkness, and re-opening their lovely petals when sunshine returns. The fascinating and innumerably-various phenomena of their morning expansion and twilight folding, are the illustrations, in part, of what botanists term the Sleep of plants. Similar phenomena occur in connection with the leaves, and together they form one of the most beautiful displays in nature of the Divine Benevolence as shown in little things.

If we examine a flower carefully, with a view to an intelligent comprehension of how it is constructed, — not necessarily pulling it to pieces, but turning it over and over, round and round, looking first at the outside, then into the depth of its heart, — we find that it consists, in the great majority of cases, of two distinct portions — an outer one, which is green, and in texture not unlike a leaf, and an inner one, which is softer than the finest satin, usually thinner than the thinnest silver-paper, and exquisitely colored. The outer portion is the "calyx," — in which word we have only another way of writing "chalice;" the inner portion is the "corolla," literally the "little crown," so called from the poetical, and therefore good and true idea which regards it as marking the day when the plant is in the enjoyment of its highest honor and glory, upon which it is "crowned," as it were, and thus in the condition of king or queen when lifted to the highest pinnacle of royal dignity by having the golden diadem placed upon the brow.

Let us look yet a little more attentively, and we

discern that this pretty flower-crown, this "corolla," is in some flowers composed of many distinct pieces or leaves, while in others it appears to consist of only *one* piece, wrought into the form of a little vase. Whether few or many, the component pieces of the corolla are called the "petals," which name, when we would speak correctly of them, we should always make use of, since the word "leaves" applies properly only to the green foliage of a plant. "Rose-*leaves*," often used for scent-pots, are properly "rose-*petals*." Now the sleep of a flower consists mainly in the changes of the positions of these "petals." The calyx or chalice which encircles them, and which covered them up while the flower was only a bud, undergoes *no* change at night, or never more than a very slight and scarcely appreciable one; the movement is confined almost entirely to the colored portion within.

And now we come to one of the most captivating chapters in the history. As there are scores of different shapes of corollas, so are there scores of different modes of closing, every different one determined by the peculiar configuration of the corolla. This is no more than we might expect from the analogies of nature, which is everywhere brimful of echoes, giving us utterances over and over again of simple and elegant ideas, that are not different intrinsically, but only presented to our eyes after another manner, just as the promises of Holy Writ are still identically the same, whether they be printed in Hebrew letters, or in English ones, or in German. Who has not noticed how various are the attitudes assumed by the different kinds of animals when they compose themselves for sleep! It is the very same thing in our own private and personal right side and left side, doublings up, stretchings out, and miscellaneous angularities;—every one of us works out some principle of ease and comfort;—every animal and every bird in like manner works out some principle of happy repose, determined, to a certain extent, by the peculiarities and the arrangement of the limbs, and signified in what we may often perhaps deem only an accidental mode, but which is original and inevitable to the creature manifesting it. Again in like manner, every flower that is so constructed as to allow of the petals changing position, has its own native, and peculiar, and invariable way of exhibiting this beautiful fact of vegetable repose. The poppy, that we spoke of just now, has four petals, which at high noon stand apart, and form a crimson bowl. When the sun sinks low in the sky, and the birds are trilling their nestward songs, the two inner petals have raised themselves so as to be upright, and have coiled themselves one round the other; the two outer petals meanwhile also lift themselves erect, but keep perfectly flat, and form a pair of great shields, one upon either side of the coil within. In the daisy, on the other hand, also in the marigold,—

> ——" that goes to bed with the sun,
> And with him rises weeping,"—

the petals are very numerous, and spread in a star-like manner round the disc of the flower. Towards twilight they all rise simultaneously, though slowly,—bring their delicate points together, and form a conical tent, which neither rain nor prowling night-insect can break through.

It is for the purpose of defending the delicate internal parts of the flower from nocturnal cold, and chill morning and evening dews, and from the ravages that might be made upon them by such of the insect tribes as come out after dark, that this admirable provision of the closing of the corolla appears to have been instituted, since there is nothing of the nature of sleep, in the human or zoological sense of the word, to be detected in plants. They do not require it. Men and women, quadrupeds and birds, seek their pillows and their various retreats when night comes on, or, at least, when they have finished their day's labor or pastime, as the case may be, because during the previous hours there has been a great expenditure of nervous energy, which requires for its re-establishment a long period of perfect physical quiescence. During sleep, the diligent little masons, carpenters, and joiners of the human body set vigorously to work, wherever repair is needed. Like an active garrison in a besieged town, they renovate during the night whatever has been damaged during the day; and when morning returns, we wake fresh, strong, and buoyant, ready to start again. Would that we were always proportionately thankful to Him who "giveth his beloved sleep," and who thus daily replaces us so comfortably on the threshold of existence! In plants there is no such expenditure of nervous energy. They have no nerves. The activity of their life is not accompanied by wear and tear. It consists solely in growth, preparation of new material, and consolidation of that material into new branches, twigs, and leaves. Whatever appearance resembling sleep they may present after nightfall, is not of the nature of slumbering repose. It is simply a relaxed condition of the petals, dependent, in most cases, upon the removal of the stimulus of the solar light, whereby they are made to subserve most elegantly the high and beautiful purpose of protecting what is at once the most important, and the tenderest, and most vulnerable portion of the flower. The centre of the flower contains the apparatus which originates the seed; and in the inmost core lies the rudimentary seed itself concealed, like the infant in its ante-natal state, almost invisible to the unassisted eye, and exquisitely sensitive to the slightest injury. It is to protect *this* that the so-called sleep of the flower is called into play. When the petals fold together, it is Nature, always solicitous to befriend, drawing the silken curtains round the cradle in which her progeny lies forming; and as nothing so much assists the growth and development of this tiny rudiment of future tree or brilliant flower as warmth, directly the sun shines again, the curtains are withdrawn, and the centre of the flower is turned as directly as possible towards the life-giving orb.

Flowers are made so beautiful as we find them, no doubt in a high degree for the delight of human eyes. Before the appearance of man upon this earth of ours, scarcely anything of the character of a flower had been ultimated into existence here. Geology makes this abundantly evident, together with the fact that flowering plants, properly so called, began to appear in plenty upon the earth's surface only when the golden period which we call the creation of man, was swiftly approaching. Human delight, however, is not their only intent. The happiness of mankind is enhanced, without question, by *every* circumstance in nature, either directly or indirectly; but a special intent in the beauty of flowers, as produced by their colored and satin-textured petals, is that they shall act as so many concave mirrors, and reflecting surfaces, catching the sun's rays, and concentrating and casting them upon the seed-forming apparatus, just as white clouds beautifully fling upon the earth light which they themselves have first received from the common source, or as silken curtains to parlor-windows transmit, when the sun is shining, a lustre not their own to our tables and books, and even to our faces.

And here it may be remarked that another use of the painted petals of flowers is to attract little flying creatures of good purpose, since, by the action of their tiny feet, and by the play of their transparent wings, they help, although unconsciously, to dislodge the pollen or yellow dust contained in the threads of the flower, and cause it to fall upon the seed-cradle, and thus help forward the production of the seed, which, unless it were fed by this yellow dust, would never come to maturity, but wither away while no larger than the point of a pin. How wonderful are the expedients made use of in so simple a thing as a flower! A flower has as many friends as a human creature. The sun, the fresh air, the dew, the nourishing earth, the rain, even the cold of winter, alike lend their aid. Bees, butterflies, a score of almost invisible pairs of wings, visit it in turn, every one of them doing its own peculiar good service.

Many flowers close their petals at nearly definite periods of the day, and others open their petals at particular times of the morning; and there are many that appear to act independently of the stimulus of light,* since they do not expand for several hours after the sun has risen. Perhaps they require the atmosphere to be well aired. There are many more, indeed, that open in the *night time*,— suggesting comparison with the birds that are nearly silent during the day, and only open their sweet throats for carols in the darkness. These have their counterparts also in moths and other insects that only fly by night, so that there is nothing in it anomalous or unnatural. Their habits cannot, indeed, be *un*natural, for they are quite as much a part of the custom and method of nature as are those of the flowers which expand with the song of the lark, or those of the birds that chant over the "morning-glories,"* or those of the butterflies that flirt their deep-dyed wings on the bosom of the rose. So exact are the times of opening and closing, that a "floral clock" may be contrived by any one who will take the trouble to collect together in a garden such flowers as are suitable, and plant them in lineal or circular order. Lin-

---

* "Morning-glories" are the flowers of the different kinds of convolvulus, all of which open at daybreak, and are remarkable for the splendor and the purity of their colors.

næus contrived such a flower-clock in his garden at Upsala, and others have been made in our own country. Of course the difference of latitude, the change of the aspect, and other circumstances, cause slight differences in the time of opening, so that no list of times drawn up in one country will exactly correspond with that of another. But they always preserve the same relation; — a particular flower is always an hour earlier or an hour later than another flower; so that when once the periods at which either of them opens, under given and definite circumstances, has been ascertained, the periods of the others may readily be calculated. It is much the same as with the positions of the stars, and their relations to particular hours of the night, according as the seasons change. Though Arcturus, and Orion, and the Pleiades, "shedding sweet influence," are not always to be found in the same part of the heavens, yet when we espy either one of them, we always know where to look for the others. The three great stars that form the slantwise belt of Orion, always point in a direct line upwards to the Pleiades; and the same three splendid diamonds always point in a direct line downwards to Sirius, the most brilliant of the fixed stars, and one of the nearest to the earth. Sirius and the Pleiades are just about equidistant from Orion's belt, so that there never need be any difficulty in determining them.

There is one large class of plants, constituting the Pea-family, in which the sleep of flowers is often accompanied by a corresponding condition of the leaves. Of course this latter is in no way subservient to the protection of the reproductive apparatus, except in a few instances, where we find the leaves that are nearest to the blossom folding together in such a way as to become a cloak for it. But this is very rare. We may observe it in the four-podded lotus; it is said to be very prettily shown also in the tamarind-tree; and those travellers in foreign countries who are quick to notice such things, have probably detected other examples. The sleep of the leaves is a simultaneous but an independent phenomenon, and its object is more like that of animal sleep, namely, to give to the vitality of the plant a respite from the employment to which it is devoted during the day, and to allow of the quiet progress of its internal or domestic economy. During the day, the leaves of plants are held in a constrained position by the force of the sunlight, which draws them towards itself as a magnet draws a piece of steel, and all this time they are diligently engaged in the preparation of new vegetable substance out of the carbonic acid, the water, and other available materials contained in the atmosphere. All this time the leaves are like so many industrious men and women, whom the morning calls away from their pillows, and impels by its inspirations to renew their daily duties. Their allegiance to the sun is precisely similar; and when, at the close of the day, the great ruler retires, and the constraint is removed, on the one hand we see the work-room and the counting-house exchanged for the arm-chair or the fireside; on the other we see the foliage that just now was spread so vividly, droop with rich and elegant languor, and lie like the ringlets on

THE SLEEP OF PLANTS.

the neck of a child that has fallen asleep in the midst of its play.

Nothing is more beautiful to contemplate than the parallel between the life of leaves and that of man. Infancy in the one is the early spring condition of the other. Each has its summer of maturity, and each has its autumn of decline; while every separate day and night is with each an alternation of activity and rest. Leaves do nothing during the night — that is to say, nothing of the nature of work for the benefit of the plant as a whole; their activity ceases when darkness comes; they never fail, however, while alive, to resume it in the morning. Nearly all that a plant contains is prepared in the leaves. The roots absorb plenty of *crude* nourishment, but it is in the leaves that this is converted into genuine plant-food; so that we may well compare them to the busy laborers who maintain the fabric and the comfort of society, — men in the town, women in the sanctuaries of home, — every one of whom who fulfils the duties of life is a leaf of the great tree of the human family. Well, too, may we expect that in the evening they should show signs of weariness, and repose themselves each in its own fashion. Man comes home to the prattle of his little folk, their tales of the day's wonders, told half out-of-breath, and with sweet dance of innocent eyes to the music of mingled voices; or he comes to the "wife of his youth," happy in her little pride, that lives not so much upon her knees as in the innermost centre of her heart, and lifts up heaven into her face in small, sweet babe-smiles that float like speech from lips yet speechless, but to call her some day by the sweetest name a woman can hear;—home he comes to these, finding that the Golden Age is not a dream of ancient poets, but a golden thread that runs through all the years and centuries, and of which he holds a filament; and over them he closes like the lotus and the tamarind.

True, it is not always so, as we may learn again from other leaves that wing-wrung and dusty, seem placed in nature only that they may supply contrasts. But, when realized, how beautiful those evening hours! Feeling and affection fill them with all forms of human delight. Is it surprising, then, is it anything but most natural, that among the changes of the green leaves, which are images of them in the world of plants, we should find the most exquisite diversities; the leaves of the lupine fold into the shape of a lady's half-opened parasol; those of the wood-sorrel dispose themselves into the form of a triangular pyramid; those of the white clover make a letter T; those of the vetch kind, which grow in opposite pairs, rise up face to face, like two hands with the palms pressed together?

We need not go into Botanic Gardens to see these things,—they lie at our feet, everywhere in the fields and woods; just as we need not go into the ranks of the rich and great to see conjugal and domestic happiness, since it is a gift equally to the poor and humble. Thus we see that a walk in the country never need be without enjoyment. Everywhere we have pretty spectacles of life in action, and like our own. And indeed it often seems as if the most wonderful illustrations were the minutest. Somehow or other, large things always seem to take care of themselves. Their bigness is a safeguard. We admire them for their grandeur, but it is hardly possible perhaps to love them so much as we love what is little; and something of the same principle seems illustrated in the ways of the Creator,— the little is always an object of consummate protection.

Lastly, as regards the sleep of flowers, it is to be observed that those in which the corolla appears to consist of only one petal, as in the foxglove, do not exhibit this beautiful phenomenon. The structure of the blossom precludes the possibility of it. Here we generally see the nocturnal protection of the stamens and pistils provided for by the peculiar shape of the corolla, and by its position. This kind of corolla is generally cave-like, or the upper part of it is in the shape of a great hood, which shoots off the rain as it falls. Very frequently also this kind of corolla is pendulous, so that in its drooping position it provides a natural self-defence for the tender parts within. Whether we can discern it or not, we may be sure that there is adequate and beautiful protection of some kind. When we think Nature has forgotten, or is partial, it is that our own eyes are dim. Moreover, there are, in all likelihood, many arrangements in nature which it is scarcely possible for eyes to make out, but which a reverent intelligence may think of from analogy, and admire as greatly as if they were visible. We do not "see" how the myriads of tiny insects find their food; but that they are all endued at once with good appetites, the satisfaction of which is a delight to them, and with abundance of good nutriment, we may be sure.

Insects.

The most populous part of the empire of Nature is that which is occupied by the various tribes of Insects. The little creatures which bear this name are the most diversified and splendidly-adorned of living things. Their histories are so romantic as to exceed the wildest flights of fancy; their habits and customs embody everything that we are accustomed to witness in the larger animals; their instincts are prophetic types of the utmost ingenuities of human reason, as brought to bear upon what ministers to our physical comfort and welfare. Many kinds furnish substances of singular excellence and beauty, such as honey, silk, and the rich crimson dye called cochineal; others are so destructive, when unchecked in their ravenous appetites and in their territorial invasions, that the result of years of peaceful growth is ruined by them almost before we are aware of the attack. And yet we are apt to pass by insects as worthless and insignificant;— we look with pleasure, it is true, upon the lovely wings of the butterfly, and upon the bees, resting on the honeyed bloom, or as they work at their amiable task with that admirable assiduity which makes them a lesson to us all, if we would "improve the shining hour;" and the sight is a fascinating one, even to the incurious, when on a warm summer's day the brilliant dragon-flies dart like winged javelins of blue steel among the grasses, and meadow-sweet, and willow-herbs that hide the margin of rural stream and river. But *other* insects, so far from being objects of interest, are for the most part disliked and hated, and it is thought very little harm to suppress them summarily with the sole of the foot. When insects are positively injurious to man, and when they infest his dwellings, of course they must be treated like other vermin. There is no more cruelty in putting certain little flat-pattern creatures to death, or in catching, if we be sharp enough, the nimble members of another race, for the same purpose, so that we may thereafter "be at rest," than there is in the trapping of foxes, or the destruction of poisonous serpents. Intelligent and kind-hearted interest in the wonderful little beings which it has pleased the All-wise to sow in such vast multitudes upon our planet, by no means requires endurance of such kinds as are offensive; our true course should be to consider the endless miracles of beauty or of adaptedness to particular purposes, which we find in Insects as a class, allowing our feelings of dislike to weigh with us only where they are really deserved.

Much, perhaps, of the popular dislike of insects arises from their being seen under circumstances at once foreign to their nature, and painful to them. Garden and rustic insects, borne unwillingly on the breeze, through open windows, into our houses, or losing their way, and entering unwittingly and probably frightened, may well appear uninteresting. They are out of place. They are like those unfortunate quadrupeds which Italian organ-boys carry about the streets. Could we see those identical monkeys in their native woods, playing forth their sprightly instincts amid the branches,— living, in a word, as nature intended them to live,— they would no longer be odious. We should perceive that the tree was made for the animal, and the animal for the tree; we should then be highly entertained and be filled with admiration. Just so, in order to form a true idea of insects, we should not think merely from the parasites and the vermin, the beetles, the meat-flies, and the wasps; nor yet from the long-legged *Tipula* that struggles against the window-panes, conscious only of its imprisonment; but from their kindred and from themselves, as inhabitants of the fields and woods and waters, their proper homes, where they are always beautiful, and which they, in turn, make more beautiful by their presence. Whoever has enjoyed the sweet and serene delight of a day in the woods, while Midsummer is saturating them with sunshine, would sadly miss one of the most charming attributes of sylvan life, were the hum of their invisible myriads to be hushed when he went again. Even the still pools and tiny lakes, which we admire for their limpid clearness, and the sweet inverted pictures that lie painted in their depths, gain perhaps a richer beauty from the eccentric dances of the water-beetles, whose polished corselets twinkle with light like that of dew-drops.

Let us, then, consider in detail a few of the facts of

Entomology. They are fully as attractive as those of Botany; and, being connected with the history of active and conscious creatures, they open our perceptions still more powerfully in regard to the inexpressible goodness of God.

We found, when considering flowers, that *protection* is a leading idea in relation to them. The same principle is manifested very wonderfully in insects, especially in the care with which the parent disposes her eggs. Few insects ever see their offspring. The blessedness of human life consists in the feast of the eyes of father and mother, when round, happy faces form a shining circle in the firelight, and proud rich hope skips twenty years for each, and fashions all that is good and noble for their destiny. Birds, that build pretty nests for their young, are probably happy in feeding the little featherless occupants. Brute creatures that give suck, have been envied before now. Even fishes, even reptiles, live some time after the birth of their progeny. But insects, excepting ants, wasps, and social bees, end their little lives unknowing either progenitor or child; every successive generation is isolated from that which precedes and follows; they exist, feed, repose, associate in love, leave eggs, and depart in peace. Moths, butterflies, and others, seldom live more than a few days after laying their eggs, and although some of their kinds do certainly survive for several months, they are only exceptions to the general rule that insects, after depositing their eggs, very soon die. We find accordingly, that the Divine Benevolence has endued the female insect with the most amazingly acute knowledge of the wants that will be felt by her unborn young, when they have no mother to direct or provide for them. The solitary bees and wasps (which constitute different races altogether from those that live in companies, and construct waxen or paper cities) labor with inexpressible industry in excavating cave-like nests in wood and stone, and in building cradles of clay, leaves, cotton, and other materials, according to their special requirements and opportunities.

Other insects, though they themselves take little or no food, and that little in the shape of honey procured from flowers, and which cannot be supposed to have any personal care about eating, deposit their eggs upon the leaves and stems of particular plants which will supply abundance of agreeable diet to the infant grubs. A third set, not satisfied with depositing their eggs in a place of safety, cover them up tenderly against the cold of winter. The female of the gypsy-moth has the lower portion of her body thickly clothed with soft down of the color of brown human hair, and with this, while laying her eggs, she forms a little bed for each, detaching the hairs with consummate ingenuity, and consuming about two days in the operation. Her partner in married life has no such down upon his body, evidently because he would find no such useful purpose to apply it to.

The brown-tail and the golden-tail moths, whose caterpillars spin warm nests for themselves before winter sets in, understand the importance also of protecting their eggs from the too-great heat of July and August, at which time they are generally laid, — excessive heat being quite as hurtful as excessive cold. They adopt precisely the same plan as that in use among the Neapolitan peasantry, who convey snow from Mount Vesuvius to Naples in the midst of summer,—covering it up in *wool*, wool being a slow conductor of heat, and preserving the snow unmelted. The female of each of these insects is possessed of a thick tuft of shining hair upon her tail, in which part she is also provided with a pair of living tweezers. The latter she employs to pluck out the former, a pinch at a time, after which she places the egg in the centre, cements it down and smooths it over. Another curious kind of defence from the rays of the sun—not however on the part of the parent, but practised by the child-insect—is one with which everybody who has ever noticed things in the country, is familiar. We allude to the oozing out of those little masses of white froth which hang so thickly upon the herbage of the hedge-banks in early summer, and in the interior of which we find the cool little tenant. This froth is popularly referred to the cuckoo, and commonly called "cuckoo-spit." The creature is green, with large and conspicuous eyes, like those which the phrenologists say are indicative of great capacity for language. When mature, it is brown, and if its tail be touched it will jump the length of a yard. In English it is called "frog-hopper," in Latin, *Tettigonia spumaria*.

The immense *capacity for enjoyment* given to every creature in some way or other, strikingly manifests itself when we consider it in connection with the insect tribes. Descending from the noble forms which enjoyment possesses in man, through the successive grades of animals below him, we still at every step find representations of it. There is not a creature unacquainted with gratification, in some shape or another. All derive it from the circumstances amid which they exist, which fact quietly suggests to us that the purest and most lasting pleasures are to be found at our very feet,— that they are not necessarily the fruit of toil and outlay, but that they flow to us out of the very nature of things, if we will but be content with what is simple and genuine. Insects, above all the minor creatures, seem to relish life. The inhabitants of the pretty shells that strew the sandy expanse uncovered by the retiring waves, adorning its brown wrinkles with sea-born jewelry, yellow, white, and pink, no doubt have their full enjoyment of existence, but one would imagine it must be marred by their exposure every time they are forsaken by the tide; the little fishes that play about in the clear water-brooks are doubtless brimful of satisfaction; the lizards on the sand-hills, glittering with green and gold; the tritons in the weedy ponds, and the small birds that hide amid the leaves, no doubt have in every instance their abundant share of animal happiness; still they none of them seem to manifest so much enjoyment as insects do. This may perhaps be accounted for, at least in part, by the fact of insects being principally — always, indeed, when in their perfect form — *aerial* creatures. In this respect they agree with birds. All things, indeed, that get much fresh air, and can sail when they like, and in whatever direction they may fancy, — through the sunshine and scented atmosphere that hangs over the green fields and sweetens the dear pastoral or healthy hills of the country — must needs have a larger and wider sensation of physical pleasure than those which are confined to the surface of the earth, or are unable to travel far from a given spot.

Do we not find it so ourselves? The foot that is familiar with the grass belongs usually to a man of lighter heart than he whose soles seldom wander from the pavement; and the best *elixir vitæ* is a run, as often as we can contrive it, amid the sweets of new and lovely scenery, where nature sits, fresh from the hands of the Creator, almost chiding us for our delay. To take special instances, however, of the enjoyment given to insects, and thus of the benevolence of Him who ordains all these good things, let us cite the dancing gnats. Every one has noticed, in calm summer evenings, what vast multitudes of these little creatures thus disport themselves. They may be traced, while the light wanes, till the eye can follow no further, and as the motions evidently serve no purpose of sustenance or reproduction, it cannot be doubted that the object is purely one of pleasure. Whenever we see the wings of insects vibrating, unless they are actually using them to pass from one place to another, we may be assured that it indicates the same kind of pleasant sensation which induces the nestling sparrow, when fed by its mother, to stretch its little pinions, and the lambkin, while sucking, to wag its tail. The birds called — from the circumstance of the movement they make when feeding — "wagtails," would seem to have a special pleasure, as members of the feathered tribes, when fulfilling this great instinct of their being. What can be more beautiful than the gayety and frolic of butterflies in the air? They frisk about, ascending, descending, moving in every possible direction, performing zig-zag pirouettes of the most elegant and varied kind, just as kittens do when upon the ground, in their more clumsy but not less sportive gambols.

Here, again, there is no purpose of direct physical utility subserved,— the movements are all tokens and expressions of pleasure. Have bees no pleasure in rambling from flower to flower, and securing the sweet spoil for the security of which they have built those beautitul little many-chambered warehouses we call honeycombs? Pleasure always attends honest and productive labor, and it would be contrary to all the analogy and harmony of nature to suppose that the bees work with no more enjoyment than a watch possesses. It is difficult to suppose that they have not indeed a pleasure in the exercise of their little wits, over and above that of collecting the floral nectar. We hardly think what excellent botanists the bees are. They do not know what "species" are, it is true; and for the matter of that, no more do our philosophers and *savans*. But they *do* know how to distinguish "genera," and may be watched going from one kind of flower to another, as cleverly as if they had received lessons from a professor.* The physical allurement of course

---

* The observation of my valued friend, Mr. R. Holland.

consists in the greater or less quantity of honey that particular kinds of flowers secrete; some producing it in large drops, others yielding only a taste. See, too, how admirably the bees are provided with instruments for procuring what they desire. Many flowers are so constructed that the bee cannot enter bodily; to meet this difficulty the little creature is provided with a long sucking-tube, which it can push far down into the blossom, so as to reach the contents.

It is beautiful to note how thoroughly the bee and the flower are adapted one to the other. They are like the old tree and the woodpecker, the fir-cone and the cross-bill; and it is wonderfully interesting, too, that in reading the records of primæval ages, held up to us by Geology, we find that it was not until flowers, essentially so named,—honey-yielding, fragrant, and painted flowers,—began to unroll their sweet petals to the sun of this world, that the little creatures we call bees were introduced as members of its animal population. Trees and plants, as well as animals, both small and great, have existed upon the surface of our planet from a past so remote that no man can speculate on the date of its beginning; but *flowers* have *not* so existed—at least there is no trace of them among the myriad fossils that are wrapped up in the rocks beneath us, while of all other parts of plants, and of organs equivalent to flowers, for the purposes of reproduction, there are abundant traces. Butterflies also would seem to be a comparatively recent dynasty. Neither they nor bees existed upon this earth very long anterior to the commencement of the human period; showing again that nothing appears in nature before it is wanted, but that all comes in at the right time, and, when its purpose is accomplished, departs. It is in this grand fitting together of things, this method, this universal adaptation and harmony of nature, that we have the best and truest external evidences of its Divine origin. The forms are superb, the colors are inexpressibly exquisite, but it is the unity of the whole that impresses us most deeply.

A few words respecting the life of insects may not be altogether superfluous. And, first, as to their changes of shape. The larger animals — quadrupeds, fishes, and birds — step into existence in their perfect forms, diminutive, it is true, but still complete; all they want is either a little more hair, or a robe of feathers, or teeth to bite with after they have been weaned, as the case may be. But insects, and several other of the lower tribes of creatures, go through a very wonderful sequence of changes. Every butterfly begins life as a grub; then it becomes a "chrysalis;" only in its third and last stage is it a winged creature. Not that the grub is metamorphosed; it contains within its soft little body the whole of the future butterfly, and, when the chrysalid condition is assumed, the butterfly often shows as plainly in it as a flower while wrapped in its calyx. In other words, the transition from the grub to the butterfly is not a "transmogrification," but a simple casting away of outer vestments, and a growth of the immature creature within to full and royal ripeness. This it is which gives so much beauty to the correspondence theologians are fond of pointing out between the life of man and his entry upon the angelic state, and the gradual development of the insect. All is in man that he will ever have; "there is a natural body, and there is a spiritual body;" the former is cast off by degrees — first the grub skin, then the chrysalid skin; lastly, the genuine immortal, who was always there, stands free and unclogged, and can mount aloft, just as the new-born-insect-angels, with their lovely wings — representative of man's new and magnificent spiritual powers when he is disencumbered of his "natural body" — soar up sunwards, our mortal eyes in vain essaying to follow.

Exceptions.

EVERYTHING that occurs in nature is the result of some law instituted to bring it to pass. No phenomena are in opposition to the laws of nature; nor are the laws of nature ever set aside in order to bring about conditions or circumstances that would be more conducive to man's welfare than the operation of the original laws themselves. Even "miracles" are no doubt in strict conformity with the primitive and immutable scheme of Divine government which has maintained the universe in its integrity and sublime order, ever since the time of that sweet aurora when "the morning stars sang together, and all the sons of God shouted for joy;" and we call them "super-natural," simply because they are effected not by suspending the laws, but by exhibiting the unaccustomed powers, of nature. For there is a spiritual law within, and thus above, every natural law, and which, being necessarily in perfect harmony with it, may dignify and expand its operation, but can never contradict it. If we feel disposed to regard miracles as works requiring the suspension of the laws of nature, it is again simply because we do not understand — and in this our present life probably cannot understand — the immensity and fulness of the laws of nature, nor see how occurrences apparently quite at variance one with another, may yet be in harmony, and be quite compatible, when viewed by the light of some grand and omnipotent principle which originates and includes both. To take a familiar illustration: every one knows that "fire burns," and that if we touch what is red hot, it will most painfully blister the skin, and that, if the contact be prolonged only for a few seconds, the flesh will be destroyed with inexpressible torment. This is the *ordinary* law of nature, and what at first sight we conceive to be the *whole* of the law of nature, with respect to the action of fire and of red-hot substances. But if a quantity of lead be melted, and made so hot that it seems incapable of any further increase of temperature, the hand may be dipped into it without sustaining the slightest injury, without being in the slightest degree burned! This is well known to chemists; and men with nerve enough to make the plunge, have many times proved it to their startled friends and pupils. This is the *extra*-ordinary law of nature; a law not in antagonism to the ordinary law, but included in the general idea and constitution of fire, part of which idea is that fire can be made so hot as *not* to burn. The miracles, and the usual order and method of nature, hold, in all probability, a similar kind of relationship, the *extra*-ordinary laws which promote the former being so administered by the Divine wisdom as to serve grand moral purposes, and this not publicly and to excite admiration, but in quiet and solemnity. Such at least is the character of the miracles recorded in Holy Writ.

When accordingly, we seem to find the common life of the world full of inconsistencies and exceptions, it is simply because we regard the several occurrences from too low a platform of thought. If such wonderful contradictions can be exhibited before our eyes as that of the melted lead burning when it is only heated enough to run like water, and *not* burning when the furnace has done its worst, or best, how readily may we believe that all other things which appear to be inconsistent one with another, are in reality in fine concord; and that exceptions are only varied utterances of some grand and simple ordinance that equally governs the common and the strange. Every department of nature presents such exceptions; and it is delightful to a reflective and pious mind to observe that these exceptions, like the sacred miracles, are uniformly charged with some errand of love, or with some new gift from the munificence of the All-good. The comfort and enjoyment, either of mankind or of some little creature, is always the proximate object; and if the end be not realized, the fault is with the intended recipient.

To begin with the inanimate or inorganic department of nature. It is well known that all substances which have been heated, as they cool decrease in size, and become of greater specific gravity; or, in other words, a little smaller, and a little heavier. Even things that are ordinarily cold, become, under the influence of severe frost, a little smaller. The strips of iron that form the path for the wheels of the railway train become shorter when the frost is intense; the pendulum of a clock, in a room where there is no fire, becomes under similar circumstances shorter, and the "time" is falsified; an iron rod that, while it is red hot, exactly fits an opening, is too small for it when it has cooled. The exception to these usual phenomena is, that *water*, one of the most valuable substances in nature, instead of decreasing in volume as it freezes, occupies more room when it has become ice; and instead of becoming heavier as it freezes, is, when in the shape of ice, perceptibly *lighter*. See how admirably this operates for the advantage of man! Had water been governed by the rule that applies to other substances, in winter, when the thermometer sunk to 32°, or "freezing point," the layer of ice formed on the surface would have immediately sunk to the bottom; another layer would have taken its place, and have similarly sunk to the bottom; and in a little while the whole reservoir would have been changed into a solid mass, which no subsequent summers could have thawed, and the world would soon have become uninhabitable for want of drink. As it is, the water is preserved in its fluid form, and warm enough for use; while the surface offers a play-ground for boy and man, agreeable in its novelty and in the excitement of the exercise needful to keep the body afloat. Sea-water does not freeze till it is nearly four degrees colder than fresh water needs to be before congealing, thus assisting to keep the ocean open at all seasons.

Mark, in the next place, the curious nature of quicksilver, or mercury. A very considerable degree of heat is required to melt every other kind of metal; but mercury becomes fluid with no more heat than is supplied by the atmosphere of England! In the Arctic regions, and wherever else the temperature sinks to —39, or seventy-one degrees below freezing-point, mercury is *solid*, resembling a lump of silver, or any other white and shining metal. There it needs fire to bring it into the fluid condition; but in our own happy island,—

"Great, glorious, and free,
First flower of the earth, and first gem of the sea,"

and in all countries of similar and even of harsher climate, so long as the intense rigor of the frigid zone is never experienced, mercury is permanently molten. Hence, we can use it for the construction of the thermometer, measuring every delicate change in the warmth of the air, and in the temperature of substances used in the processes of arts and manufactures, which could scarcely be attempted without the aid of this wonderful instrument. Quicksilver is one of the most extraordinary substances in nature. It supplies one of the deadliest of poisons, and one of the most potent of medicines. It is the delight of children, as its globules roll prettily up and down the tea-tray, chasing one another like themselves in their swift-footed sports, and reflecting every happy little face that peers into their tiny yet brilliant mirrors; man sees in it an emblem of the heavenly flock that in this present life is broken into particles innumerable, kept asunder by the dust, the hindrances, the misunderstandings, the infirmities of the life in the body, but which are yet all of one substance and purpose, spherical and bright, in their souls; and which, though the sport of the world, and called by many names,—Ephesian and Laodicean, Episcopalian and Independent,—shall yet resolve, when assembled by Him who sitteth as the Refiner and Purifier, into glorious and everlasting unity.

One other illustration from the inorganic world, and we conclude. While quicksilver melts with the first kiss of solar warmth, *platinum* defies the utmost heat of the crucible. Hence, by the art of the welder, it can be manufactured into little cups and other vessels that are required to endure the intensest fire, serving purposes of recondite chemistry which without it could never be achieved.

In the *vegetable* kingdom this admirable arrangement attracts us at all points. The idea of a plant, when developed with all its parts complete, includes root, stem, leaves, flowers, and seed. But every one of these parts is at times found to be wanting, so far as palpable and visible reality is concerned; some plants being exceptionally destitute of root, others of stem, others of leaves, &c. The absence of the respective parts gives an exquisite variety and gracefulness to the face of nature, such as no poet can describe, and no painter depict on his canvas. Were plants always anchored to the ground by genuine roots, the mistletoe would hang no golden bough amid the gray and tattered thorns and apple-trees of mid-winter, a crowd of living pearls entangled amid branches that wear the semblance of death; no lichens would enrich the old tower and dismantled castle with time-stains of purple and orange that make the deep sheen of the faithful ivy yet more lustrous in its contrasted verdure; nor would orchids dwell, like birds, amid the boughs of tropical trees, adorning the vigorous one with rich hues, and scenting it with composite and warm aroma, alike foreign to its personality, and rendering the decrepit far more beautiful in decay than it stood even in the prime of its existence. The orchids are well known to the lovers of choice flowers. After the forget-me-not, the maiden-hair fern, and the pretty uncurling leaves of our own old-fashioned English ferns, comforted with brown plumage till they are strong and tall, there are none that form such links of pleasure between the giver and the receiver. It is not, however, so well known that in their native woods they are strictly *aerial* plants,— that is to say, that they perch themselves in the clefts of the boughs, deriving their nourishment from the air and from the decaying organic matter that lodges around them, and that, if planted in earth, many of them will not live.

Of *stemless* plants we have examples in innumerable field flowers, and in many flowers of the garden, such as the tulip and the crocus. They have flower-stalks, certainly, but they have no proper *stem*. To this class of plants is mainly owing the sweetly-variegated vesture that conceals the soil, providing turf in the meadow and lawn, embroidery for them when summer comes, and tapestry of moss for the flanks of the waterfall. Fancy the aspect of a country where the earth was perennially like a street, or a newly-ploughed field, or a newly-gravelled garden-walk, and the figment will be that of a world without stemless plants;—the flowers and the fruit aloft, reserved for men; no sea of daisies for the tiny ones in spring; no loved small hands overflowing with bluebell and wood anemone—to a child the blossoms of paradise itself. Among the stemless plants are many *acrid* ones. The herbage of the fields is by no means the exclusively sweet and juicy fodder we may deem it. Buttercups are quite the reverse of sweet. The pastoral animals eat but few of them, and then apparently as condiments to the succulent and insipid grass, just as we ourselves take pepper and salt to our meat and potatoes. How beautiful, again, the exception in regard to many of those low-growing plants, when specially and directly serviceable to man, that, unlike the enduring Trees,—those great, grand pillars which watch the rise and fall of generations,— *they last only for a year.* Wheat, barley, peas, beans, turnips, carrots, if not annual, are only biennial. They must be sown fresh and fresh every year; so that man, instead of living without employment; thence lapsing into indolence; thence into evils, from which occupation preserves him, as he would most certainly do, did his daily bread drop off trees into his mouth, like acorns on to the pigs' refectories in the woods—instead of this, is kept continually engaged, tilling the soil, depositing the seed, reaping, threshing, grinding, baking. These occupations call others into play. The general stimulus to all the powers of the mind shows itself in inventions, art, and sciences; and to the exceptional circumstance of the staff-of-life growing upon an annual instead of a perennial plant, man may ascribe, under Providence, a large measure of his civilization, the best temporal sign of which is the neatness and completeness of his breakfast and dinner table arrangements. As the moral culture of a community may always be judged of by its treatment of women, so may the civilization of a people or nation by the mode in which it takes its food.

Further, it is noticeable among these little plants of the fields, that, while most of the members of the vegetable kingdom give out such odor as they may have power to *during life*, the vernal-grass, the woodruff, and others, are not fragrant till they have been torn away from their roots, and have begun to get dry. The rose, the lilac, the Daphne, and the acacia, pour forth their perfume as a part of their day's duty. The woodruff, that holds up handfuls of little white crosses in the pleasant woods and shady glens, yields no scent till its life has ebbed — beautiful emblem of those who delight us while they live, out of the serene abundance of their kindly hearts, but whose richer value we only begin to know when they are gone away, and of whose white souls we then say inwardly, "He, being dead, yet speaketh." So the hay-field, that rolls like sea waves, is scentless when we pass it uncut; we hear the measured *sweesh* of the scythe, death lays each green head low, and odor rises like mist.

The tall trees have their exceptional brethren no less than the dwarf plants. Some, instead of denuding themselves when autumn comes, keep their leaves all through the winter. We call them "evergreens," and at Christmas decorate our houses with their cheerful branches. Save for their green solace, the world would look very bleak and bare; as it is, the exception passes us comfortably through the sense of winter, and we feel over again that no deluge is ever so dreadful but that some little ark still floats upon the water, and keeps life and hope intact. Look at that venerable lime-tree! All other trees spread their branches far and wide, and, as long as they live, if we go under them, and cast our eyes upwards, we can see more or less of the sky, or at least there is plenty of room for us to climb; but the interior of an aged lime-tree is filled with little twigs, that form quite a brushwood. This impervious labyrinth offers a secure asylum for the smaller birds, when pursued by hawks; once inside, they can never be got at, and can rest, and go forth at will to renew their minstrelsy. Thorny trees and bushes, which also are exceptional to the general structure of plants, offer similar asylums to little birds.

The *rule* is that leaves shall be *green*. Wherever we cast our eyes, the prevalent hue is that of the grass, unless when burned-up by the scorching heat of summer, or concealed by the white snow-mantle of Christmas, and even then we are reminded of it by the laurel, the holly, and other trees which are not forsaken by their foliage in October. But the leaves of some plants and trees are *not* green. When, for instance, the garden amaranths creep out of the ground, they are of a fine, lively red; and this color they retain in every part of their fabric till they die. In good greenhouses and conservatories there are many such plants, *i. e.*, plants dyed of some strange rich hue which quite upsets the definition of a plant as "a *green* thing." Nature will not allow herself to be defined. When we think we have constructed our definitions so carefully that they are accuracy itself, and have marked out our boundaries and dividing lines, and then, quitting our chairs, go abroad into living nature, the work is found to have been vain; some odd plant or animal, as the case may be, is sure to be detected walking through the fences; we invariably discover that we only "know in part;" and when the larger knowledge has been obtained, and we again compare our schemes with nature, still it is the same,—mystery within mystery, hill behind hill, more and yet more islands in the infinite archipelago of truth and wonder.

Among the most beautiful of these painted-leaf-plants are the various kinds of Begonia, which upon the under side are often of a deep claret color, while the upper surface is marked with silvery spots and arches. Some kinds of Caladium have their leaves exquisitely dyed in the centre with crimson; others have crimson spots and blotches. The young leaves of the Dracæna are rose-color; those of certain Crotons are variegated with rose and yellow. All this is quite exceptional, and the peculiarity is accompanied in most cases by another, namely, the comparative insignificance of the flowers of these painted-leaved plants. It would seem that the grand principle of equal gifts to every living creature was here intended to be palpably illustrated. Where the foliage is plain and simple, green without inlay of purple or other tint, the flowers are in most cases showy and ornamental; where, on the other hand, the foliage is so deeply enriched that it looks more like flowers, then the actual blossoms are ordinarily of little pretension. Everywhere in nature is this kind distribution maintained. The man who is clever in languages is often inapt for physical science; when the hand can execute beautiful drawings, or make dull wires and woodwork give forth delicious music, there is often inaptitude for metaphysics. Every one has something bestowed which, if faithfully and honorably cultivated and diffused, shall be the admiration of another; no one need *envy*, for he has that in himself which is also enviable, if he will only be true to his own powers and duties. These pretty plants with their deep-hued leaves, need not sigh for the blossoms of the camellia or the tulip; they are in themselves, though relatively flowerless, a banquet for all taste and capacity of delight.

Lastly, a few words upon remarkable exceptions in connection with animals. Most creatures reside permanently in their native countries; but some kinds change their quarters every spring or autumn, going to warmer or cooler regions, according as their instinct of self-protection prompts them. Hence, in early summer, our ears are saluted with the sweet cry of "Cuckoo!" Hence, in winter, we see birds of northern origin, Scandinavian strangers, little claws that have clung to Lapland birches, and wings that have flapped near icebergs. What tales of travel, were they gifted with words! One of the most useful of birds gives us *eggs*.

When these are boiled, the contents coagulate, and become pleasant food; all other things, when boiled, become *soft*.

When we contemplate the organic provision made for the nourishment of her young by the female animal, we find it numerically proportioned to the number of her offspring at a birth, or to the occasional number. Woman has two breast-fountains, the cow has *four;* yet the progeny of the cow is rarely increased by more than two at a time, and usually by only one. The exceptional excess is, apparently, for the use of man; for whose service also the bees store a larger quantity of nectar than they require for their own consumption; and the law, "flowing with milk and honey," is shown to be a far-thought-of gift of the Divine Benevolence. Woman is exceptional to all other animals in her matchless capacity of nurse to her young. All other creatures that give suck, soon wean their offspring, and leave them to shift for themselves. Not so the most sacred servant of God. In those long yet patient hours when we lie, poor, helpless, thankless little things, wailing in the darkness; loved the more tenderly, pressed the more closely to our infant home, white as a snow-drop, and warm as the heart's best life-blood — ah, what a river of affection bursts from its heavenly spring, pouring on past all the years, believing all that is good and noble, and ever listening for it — forgiving all that is weak and erring, pleading till the heart well nigh breaks that the disobedient may be turned to the wisdom of the just; for it is love that would surrender life itself rather than enter heaven desolated "because they are not." A mother's love is distinguished from all others in this, that it overruns, from the beginning, time and the world, and looks to the eternal home where both shall live forever.

Chemistry.

HITHERTO we have given our attention almost exclusively to the objects and phenomena of living nature; we will now look for a little while at the marvellous discoveries of chemistry, that magnificent science which unfolds the laws and composition of the inorganic and inanimate portion of the world. Chemistry, in its wonderful disclosures, and the experiments by which we are made familiarly acquainted with its principles, approaches so nearly to "magic," that had some of the more curious knowledge of to-day been possessed by the philosophers of the middle ages, they would assuredly have been dealt with as sorcerers. In an enlightened age, men, if they cannot follow the quick steps of those who lead, still admire their powers and achievements; in a dark age, the speed and insight are attributed to some supernatural and perhaps unholy aid, and the true and beautiful become objects of hatred and persecution; just as in all ages, in regard to theology and all the highest truths connected with man's eternal welfare, that which a man sunk in sensualities of necessity cannot see the fulness and radiance of, seems to him, contrariwise, only black and unprofitable error.

It is possible to freeze water in a red-hot crucible, letting the lump of ice fall out upon the table while the vessel in which it was formed still glows with the action of the fire; it is possible to produce upon a parlor-table light that shall seem brilliant as a fragment of sunbeam; it is possible, yea, and very easy, to prepare a powder that on being shaken out of the glass tube in which it is preserved, takes fire, atom by atom, simply by coming in contact with the air! One of the simplest and prettiest experiments for winter-evening amusement by the fireside is the setting lumps of a certain metal in a blaze by merely touching them with a drop of cold water! Had these things, we repeat, been exhibited when men who had science and thought enough to discover the wonders of nature were impeached of communication with the powers of darkness, what would have been the result and their fate! Many have suffered imprisonment and stripes for the promulgation of truths and discoveries not so wonderful. Let us be thankful that the Divine wisdom withholds the knowledge of such things till mankind is able to receive it reverently, neither suspecting the origin nor buffeting the instrument, and is able moreover to apply it to high practical uses, at once inviting the imagination to further inquiry, and supplying new proof of the Benevolence that everywhere guides and overrules.

This Benevolence shows itself in inorganic nature under two principal forms, viz., the composition of substances, and their action and reaction upon one another. The presence of every primary element can instantaneously be detected; and if it be a poisonous substance that we are dealing with, we know pretty well how to neutralize the baneful operation it would exert. Although when we look at nature in the mass, the materials of which it is composed seem infinitely diversified, and, practically, no doubt are so, yet on analyzing them, we find that the absolutely different elements do not exceed seventy. It is much the same with the composition of the world as with that of language. There are scores, yea, hundreds of thousands of different words in constant utterance by mankind in their various countries. English alone has tens of thousands of words in it; yet how few are the letters of the alphabet that are required for their construction! By varied intermixture of the simple twenty-six letters which form our first lesson at school, all that is needful for daily talk is produced — all that is needful to express the highest and loveliest sentiments, the most recondite propositions, the most brilliant insights of poetry. First, these little letters are combined into syllables; the syllables are united in twos and threes; they are variously arranged, multiplied and repeated, and an inexhaustible vocabulary is the result. It is precisely the same with the composition of the objects of nature. The seventy primitive elements correspond to the twenty-six alphabetical sounds and characters. Some, like *q* and *z*, occur comparatively seldom; other elements, like *a* and *e*, are incessantly in demand.

The first result of the mixture of these elements is found in water, lime, salt, soda, &c. When these are blended, entirely new compounds result; and the blending of these again, gives the infinitely diversified materials the analysis of which introduces the chemist to the mysteries of his fascinating science. The bodies of all animals, trees, plants, and flowers are similarly compounded of a few of the primitive elements, by successive processes of combination, the new compounds often presenting few or no traces of the qualities which marked their atoms before being united. Man is well called the "noblest work of God." Aristotle defined him as the "imitative animal;" other philosophers have called him the "cultivating," the "bargain-making," the "cooking" animal; the chemist describes him as an elaborate compound of carbon, nitrogen, water, lime, and phosphorus, with a little iron, &c., superadded; and reduced to the ultimate analysis, in truth, his material body is nothing besides, since the blood, the muscles, the bones, the nails, and the hair, are only so many exquisite mixtures, prepared by the agency of Life direct from Him in whom we move and have our being, and moulded by the fingers of infinite wisdom into shapes of absolute perfection, and of incomparable adaptedness to the noble purposes for which they are designed. Similarly, the lovely and fragrant rose is composed of no more than carbon and water, some ammonia, and perhaps a little iron; and, when disintegrated in the chemist's laboratory, can be presented as a few grains and drops of colorless relic.

How wonderful the guiding and controlling power that, out of dull and inanimate materials such as these, can weave shapes so transcendently beautiful, filling them with energy to perform their comely uses, and, when those uses have been fulfilled, and they die, causing other things to rise from their ashes! For it is not only a fact that the objects of nature are made out of a *few* elements — they are positively made out of identically the same particles, taking turn with one another. There is no reason to suppose that a single atom of matter has been added to material nature since it pleased the Creator to dispose it in its present form; it is certain that not a single atom has passed out of existence; in other words, the bulk and weight of our planet and its enveloping atmosphere are precisely the same to-day that they were thousands of years ago, when things "began," whatever the date of that beginning; and yet during those multitudinous years, countless millions of plants and animals have run their little race of life, have died, decomposed, and returned to the dust. Where has the material come from? It has been simply the old material. Every atom has done duty over and over again; to-day entering into the composition of a tree or flower, next year into that of an animal; after that, perhaps wandering in the air for awhile; by-and-by re-appropriated into the fabric of a plant or bird; in fact, enduring like a piece of money, unaltered in itself, but passing incessantly from place to place: to-day — resuming the metaphor of the coin — a widow's mite, to-morrow part of the heaped-up treasures of a Crœsus. Our very breath is of this nature. The atmosphere we inhale is not of original English birth, nor does it abide permanently in England. Part of it has been sifted through the branches of the cedars of Lebanon; part of it has been moistened with the spray of the unpastured sea, a thousand leagues from where we stand; when we have done with it, by degrees it will move away, on the wings of the wind, to supply nutriment to people of whom we know nothing but that they live, and to many a blossom "born to blush unseen." In its history it is an image, viewless, but faithful as if wrought in perfect marble, of the whole economy of material nature, vicissitudes, wanderings, and transformations, all included. No portion is ever lost; and though the whole never comes again intact, we have it renewed without ceasing.

Let us now cite a few examples of the operation of the Divine Benevolence with respect to the power given to man to detect the various elements of nature. Every substance is discoverable by some "test," which usually neutralizes it, or rather, which by uniting with it, forms a new compound. The whole fabric of chemistry rests upon this wonderful principle, as one of its corner-stones. Thus, if the least fragment of copper be dissolved in acid, and the fluid be then diluted with water until no trace of color remains, so potent, nevertheless, is the affinity of *ammonia* for the copper, that a single drop of the latter fluid will immediately reveal the presence of the metal, by uniting with it, and forming a new substance of the loveliest violet color. Similarly, if a morsel of lead be dissolved in acid, and the acid be then diluted with water, a single drop of a solution of *iodide of potassium* will turn the whole to a brilliant crocus-yellow. The presence of iron, after the same manner, is discovered by the least drop of tincture of galls, which blackens it upon contact; that of silver by a little solution of common salt, which causes flakes of imitative snow to make their appearance; that of mercury again with iodide of potassium, which turns the fluid containing it to a beautiful red. Every one of these tests is *reciprocal;* that is to say, we discover the presence of galls by administering a little solution of iron; and of ammonia by introducing a little copper. The test for zinc is remarkably curious. A drop of ammonia causes a white cloud in the watered solation of the metal, but in a few moments, if we shake it, the cloud dissolves, and the fluid becomes clear and limpid as before! The value of these simple facts to the science of chemistry cannot possibly be over-estimated. Every substance, in the hands of the magician of the laboratory, is a new Spear of Ithuriel, extorting confession on the instant of the character of that which is touched with it; and as no two results of "testing" in different directions are absolutely alike, the chemist is provided with an infallible clue to all the realities of the composition of things. How grand and inexhaustible does the Divine Wisdom appear, when we discover the humblest and commonest substances in nature to be connected by ties of affinity which a little child may bring to light; which are yet so mysterious as to captivate the philosopher, at the same moment that they provide him with his initial keys of knowledge. By means of these "tests," we can detect all kinds of mineral *poisons.* No deadly substance can lie so deeply concealed as to evade answer when called. Hence the difficulty, now-a-days, of administering poison without discovery. Though months may have elapsed after the commission of a murder by mineral poison, the traces may be found; some "test" will declare what has been done, and what kind of poison has been employed. Along with this there **is** another great fact to be considered. **The** "tests" which prove the presence of the poison often possess the power, if used in time, of neutralizing **its** effect. **This is** the case with oxalic acid, a deadly poison **not** infrequently given by mistake **of** ignorant people for Epsom **salts.** A small quantity of limewater being added, the **acid** and **the** earth combine, **a** white powdery **substance is formed in** a moment, **and** this, being insoluble, is perfectly harmless. So with **the** burning and corrosive fluid called sulphuric acid, **one of the** most important **of known** substances, **alike for** the purposes of chemistry and for those of many **of the** useful **arts.** If **a drop be spilled** upon the table **or** upon the fingers, **the instant that a similar drop of any** solution **of** the **earth called baryta is added to it, the** burning property is neutralized, **and** we have a milk-white product incapable of doing harm.

No man need complain of the existence in this world of so many hurtful and deadly things, when he reflects **how ready** and certain **are** the antidotes. Wherever **there is an evil**, there is always for the intelligent mind some compensating good. No winter is so cold but its asperities are outbalanced **by the** sweets of summer. While the nettle is preparing the sharp sap that makes its sting so virulent, the dock is preparing another sap that shall assuage the pain. In chemistry we see more perhaps of this grand principle than in any other department of natural knowledge, **since the effects are** here at once instantaneous, varied almost without end, and impossible to be misconceived. It brings palpably before us, over again, the fewness and the universality of the principles of the Divine government; all phenomena resulting in manifestations of bountiful care for the happiness and health of man, and all the phenomena of the natural world, being no other than the economic laws of the moral world played forth in pictures and representations. See, again, how beautifully the union of chemical elements, when placed in juxtuposition, becomes subservient to the highest purposes of human sympathy, in connection with invisible writing! When the remnant of English troops, left after the disasters at Cabool, some fifteen years ago, were shut up in a fort, surrounded and vigilantly watched by their enemies, they managed nevertheless to send brief letters to their nearest friends. These letters to appearance were only blank pieces of paper. But they were covered with words traced with rice-water instead of ink, every word becoming visible in bright blue when the paper was washed over with iodine! This wonderful substance, iodine, has the property of turning starch blue or violet color; and as rice contains a considerable quantity of starch, an invisible ink prepared from it assumes that hue when touched with iodine, though previously quite colorless. Eventualities, such as the imprisonment adverted to, are quite as much a part of the system of nature as the most ordinary occurrences, and all are anticipated in these simple and beautiful laws.

The nourishment of our bodies consists in a series of

chemical actions. Some portion of our food goes to the formation of flesh and blood; another portion contributes to the substance and solidity of the bones; a third portion is *fuel*. In this latter contrivance we have a most striking illustration of the simplicity and perfection of the Divine ordinances. There is no life without warmth, and warmth comes of the combination of certain elements, a process incessant in the human body, and consisting in no more than the chemical union of "oxygen" and "carbon"—the latter the chief constituent of fat, and the former inhaled continuously as part of the air. Every time we breathe we quicken the burning of the "flame of life," which is thus maintained quite unconsciously. When we "hold our breath," we thereby slacken the supply of oxygen; and when we cease to take food, we reduce the supply of carbon, each being equally requisite with the other to maintain the cheerful glow that we call our animal heat. Thus is one of the most agreeable sensations of life a simple result of chemical action, the materials broken up into atoms so minute as to be invisible to the most powerful microscope, but all obeying the great behest that all things shall work together for the comfort of the world and of mankind, and thus for the glory of Him who hath created them "for His pleasure."

The Dispersion of Plants upon the Face of the Earth.

TRAVELLERS, on their return from the exploration of distant countries, tell us of every conceivable diversity of climate and of terrestrial surface. Those who have penetrated the Arctic circle describe snows almost perennial, and a region so inhospitable that everything necessary to support human life must be carried thither; those who bring home the browned faces that show the intensity of Indian sunshine tell of arid and sandy plains from which every particle of moisture appears to have been evaporated long ages ago. Some give us accounts of huge mountains where, at midsummer, the white mantle of mid-winter still lingers undissolved, though at the base it is fervid summer, all latitudes being represented in miniature during the course of a few thousand feet of vertical ascent; others, again, tell us of countries where rain does not fall for a dozen years at a time, and where the surface of the ground is covered with crystallized salts. Wonderful is this, whatever the associations under which it is regarded; more wonderful yet is the fact that every spot of earth, hot or cold, high or low, is supplied with vegetation at once appropriate and ornamental. No place is incapable of supporting vegetable life of *some* kind; and although there are districts where grass and trees are never seen, and perpetual desolation gives the idea of their being worn-out and effete, as happens in the great deserts in the interior of northern Africa — even there it is not so much an absolute incapacity to sustain life, as the want of springs of water that causes the absence of it. In those sweet spots which have become a metaphor for all happy and blessed breaks in the history of trouble and sorrow, — the "oases" of the desert, — water is present, and vegetation is triumphant. Such an "oasis" was Elim, where "there were twelve wells of water, and threescore and ten palm-trees."

How marvellous, then, in our eyes, does that Divine power and wisdom again become, which provides a fitting vesture of plant and flower for every spot of earth, yea, and a vegetable population for every stream and pond of water, for every lake and every sea, whether salt or tasteless. Hot springs have their vegetable inhabitants no less than cold rivers and chilly cascades. The driest acres of Arabia have plants congenial to them, no less than the broad plains of happy islands like our own, where in spring we may watch "from field to field the vivid verdure run." It does but carry out beautifully and intelligibly before our very eyes that the Creator not only formed and created the earth, but formed it "to be inhabited." The idea of "habitation" may seem to signify families of *mankind*, and no doubt it does so in the first and inmost meaning, but a large and philosophical and reverent reading of the text, will connect with it the families also of the humbler portion of living nature, or animals in all their variety, and not animals only, but the families of trees and plants. All these has HE created "for his pleasure," and though we may not understand the mode and the degree of their ministration, still may we be assured that the flourishing existence of crowds of happy animals—happy, that is, in the enjoyment of their peculiar life—and of myriads of blooming and lovely plants, is an integral part of that Divine pleasure; and thus that the races, in all their diversity, of quadrupeds and birds, fishes, and all the little denizens of earth and sea, together with those of all plants, are essentially included in the general term of inhabitants of our planet, and were given to it in order that they might dwell upon it and decorate it. In the present paper we shall endeavor to show that the connection of plants with the surface of our earth is in no respect a less admirable fact than that of their existence, and that the laws and arrangements by which the connection is maintained, rank with the most striking in any department of the science of nature.

The great physical stimuli of vegetable growth are light and heat—a noteworthy fact when regarded in relation to the correspondence that light and heat bear to the exciting and sustaining physical forces of which we every day feel the glory as Divine wisdom and Divine love. Where there are most heat and light, trees and flowers of all kinds are most plentiful and most splendid—always provided that there is an adequate supply of moisture; where **heat and** light **are** deficient, there **we see poverty and dwarfishness. In** the **tropics the forests are more** majestic **than any one** accustomed **only to** the woods of northern **Europe can** possibly **conceive, many of** the **trees clothing themselves with** leaves as **large as** dinner-tables; **while the** flowers that **are poured forth from** every branch **and** twig **are finer than lilies. By people coming from the** extreme north, on **the other hand,** our **English** lilacs **and** laburnums **are regarded as miracles of size and** loveliness; **for** in **the frigid zone, although there are** "flowering plants" **with** hard and woody stems, **answering so far to the idea of shrubs, they never rise more than** a few inches above the ground. **Dr. Clarke brought from Scandinavia six full-grown birch-trees in his pocketbook; and the** greater **part of the Arctic willow is to be found, not in the air, but below the surface of the soil! It is much the same at the extreme south of the great American continent. Near Cape Horn, trees** which in latitudes **a** little warmer **allow of the traveller walking** *underneath* **them, become so** diminutive, **and stand so** thick together, as he ascends the mountain **higher and higher,** that at **last** he may walk **upon their tops!**

It is very **important** to observe **here that it is the** *combined* **agency of** light and heat **that produces the wonderful results** seen **in the tropics, again inviting our** minds to the **contemplation of the grand correspondence** above alluded to. **Clear and** brilliant light **often** brings **out** exquisite colors, as happens among **the Alps** and also in the north frigid **zone, where the** humble little plants called lichens and mosses are in many cases dyed of the most brilliant hues, purple and gold predominating. Warmth, in like manner, will stimulate vegetable growth in the most astonishing manner, but it is growth not necessarily accompanied by the secretion of valuable substances, such as give quality and real importance to the plant. In English hot-houses, for example, we have abundance of spice-trees, those generous plants that yield cinnamon and cassia, the nutmeg and the clove; but although healthy and blossoming freely, they never mature their aromatic secretions. Though they have artificial heat equal to that of their native islands, which burn beneath the sun of the Indian Ocean, we cannot supply them with similar and proportionate solar *light*. Our cloudy skies shut us in from the full and direct radiance of the sunshine, and wanting this, heat alone will not avail.

Next to be considered, as greatly influencing the distribution of plants over the surface of the earth, is the varying height of its different portions above the level of the sea. It is a very interesting fact, and one familiar to those who travel much, even within the area of the British Islands, that the plants of lofty mountains are, to a considerable extent, quite different from those which enamel the fields that lie at their feet; the cold, the damp, caused by their frequent immersion in the clouds, and the rarer atmosphere, being congenial to different kinds. Mounting the steep slopes of Snowdon or Helvellyn, we soon come to vegetable forms that are never seen in the lands below; and in Scotland the number of such new forms is again greatly

THE DISPERSION OF PLANTS. 69

augmented. In warm countries, on the **other hand**, it is very **curious to** observe how close is **the** agreement between **a** certain number of yards of vertical elevation, **with the** departure so many degrees north **or south** from the equator. **On the** mountain-chain of which Mount Ararat is the most important geographical point, **all the** varieties of vegetation **betwen** Syria **and the** North Pole may be observed by any one patient enough to ascend from base to summit. **At** the foot of **Mount Ararat** there are the **vine,** the **olive** and the fig, **the** palm also, **and the** orange. A little **way up, these** fruits cease **to** ripen, **and** their place is taken **by the** trees **and plants of** central Europe ; **a** little further, again, those of Russia **and** Norway **make their appearance ;** by-and-by **the vegetation of Scandinavia becomes predominant, and the crown of the** mountain **is lost in unmelting snow—a North Pole** reached **by vertical** ascent instead of **by a long journey through** seventy **degrees of** latitude. **The analogy of** a great snow-**capped** mountain in **any tropical country** with either **the northern** or southern hemisphere is most complete. **The** base answers **to** the equatorial zone ; the middle portion answers to the temperate ; **and** the summit an-**swers** to the frigid. In a word, our planet **is** like two vast tropical mountains sliced off at the **base, and so** conjoined as to let their summits be the **two poles, the** arctic and the antarctic respectively.

Soil, and the geological composition of the ground below, have also great influence upon the vegetation of a district ; for plants, like animals, have their appropriate **food.** True, to the great **mass of** plants, it is a question of little moment. They grow freely in every kind of soil, and hence the colored fantasy of the fields, in which plants grow inextricably mingled. It remains true, nevertheless, that many kinds require certain mineral constituents in the soil, in order that they may attain perfection; while others prefer certain geological formations, on account of the easier drainage or the greater retentiveness of water. It is interesting to see how the plants of widely-separated districts often agree, when the soil is the same, or nearly so. Many of the wild-flowers, for example, of St. Vincent's Rocks, at Clifton, are seen but sparingly, or not at all, after we quit Gloucestershire on our way northwards, until we come close upon the sea-margin of North Wales. Then they are found again, and save for the new landscape, we might almost fancy ourselves breathing the soft sweet air of Durdham Down. The rocks and soil of these two districts are in many respects closely similar, and their products illustrate the harmony that so often subsists between the earth and vegetation. It is no small part of the Divine Benevolence thus to distribute and marshal the substances and objects of nature; for to the exiled and expatriated there are sweet and fond sights produced as a consequence of it, that oftentimes make amends for the severance, and, by association, import the distant into the present. What an inducement, moreover, to the study of nature! If the sound of a national melody heard in a far-distant land awaken all tender recollections of the dear fields so many leagues away, no less so does the spectacle of the trees and flowers that were the delight of our youth, when we behold them in the remote spot of our adoption. Anything whatever that animates the soul with a secret pleasure, whether it come through the medium of sight or of sound, of poetry, or science, or philosophy, of thought or of reading, or of intercourse with our fellowmen, or, though last not least, of the little wild-flowers, is a fine expression and result of the Divine Benevolence in little things, in which we should rejoice and for which we should be grateful. One of the most beautiful and ennobling of all joys and satisfactions is the joy of being grateful to God; and nothing makes us more truly human than the accustoming ourselves to find reasons for and inducements to such joy in the little and miscalled "insignificant" and trifling things of nature. All are made for our personal enjoyment, and to help us onwards into manliness and humanity of spirit, and they will effect that result if we will open our hearts to their influence.

Very curious indeed are the special arrangements by which the seeds of plants are conveyed from place to place, thus providing for the permanency of the green carpet. Many kinds are provided with delicate feathery wings, which the wind soon seizes upon, carrying them for miles over the country. Every one in the heavenly era of early youth has blown the little ships from the dandelion into the aerial sea, curious merely to learn the time of day, and unconscious that by this little pastime the great purposes of nature were being assisted. It is true that in many of the plants which have these winged seeds, we do not recognize any special usefulness to man; and the means provided for their wide dispersion may look like good labor bestowed to little genuine purpose of benevolence; but we are not to judge of the usefulness of a thing by what it yields directly and immediately to *man*. The population of the earth includes millions of creatures besides ourselves, and anything that seems useless to *us* is no doubt invaluable to some other race. Here it may be remarked too, in passing, that the existence of so-called "useless things" is one of the grand proofs of another and nobler state of being. They are outbirths of a nobler world, and have a destiny and purpose of their own; if they are useless in *our* eyes, they may be of great use in the eyes of *other* creatures of God — if not in this outer world, yet in the inner one where their spiritual forms exist, and whence they operate. Birds and insects carry seeds about almost as busily as the wind. The rough and hairy coats of quadrupeds often come in contact with and capture the burrs of certain plants, which thus get conveyed unintentionally for thousands of miles, or even half round the globe. Rivers and all running waters perform a similar use; multitudes of plants are found growing upon their banks, the seeds of which have been brought by the current from distant localities, and being stranded when the water is low, they find at once an anchorage and an abiding-place for growth. There are even plants that can jerk and dart out their seeds like shots from tiny guns, for the purpose of their wider dispersion! Touch-me-nots and cardamines form quite a miniature artillery when ripe, discharging their little batteries with a vigor that is quite facetious. All these things, let us never forget, are special arrangements for promoting the beauty of the world, **for** clothing it with green **and graceful** life, and for thus carrying out **the** designs of Infinite Wisdom and Infinite **Love.**

The water, like the land, is filled with vegetation,— that **is,** everywhere except **in the open sea, and even** there may often be found abundance **of the** strange marine **plants** called Algæ. Half-way across **the Atlantic there is an enormous submerged forest of one** kind in particular, called "gulf-weed," from **its** connection with the **great "gulf-stream"** that **makes its** way **from** the Gulf of Mexico. **This mass of** weeds **is so** dense **as sometimes to** impede **the** progress of **ships; and when encountered by** Columbus, **in that** wonderful exploring voyage westwards which **was rewarded by** the discovery **of the** sentinel-islands **of America, it was** thought **by** the superstitious **sailors to be a** barrier **specially placed there by** an **angry Providence, to prevent their** further passage, **or at all events to warn them from** prosecuting the **attempt to cross the sea. Similarly, in** the remotest **portions of the** antarctic **ocean,** there are prodigious sea-weeds with **stems of the girth of a man's body, and** branches that extend through the water **to an** almost indefinite distance. Our English coasts show **two** classes of **these** curious and interesting plants. **First, there are the dark leathery** weeds which form **tapestry for the sea-washed cliffs, and** float so beautifully **in the foamy water when the tide comes up** to salute them. Secondly, **there are the** lovely green **and** rose-colored **weeds that are seldom more** than a few inches in length, and which we may see lying about on the sands like fragments of roses, or in exquisite arabesque of pink fibres. Were we to seek them in their native habitats, or while growing, we should find them erect and displayed, forming a parterre for the sea, in its way no less lovely than are the flower-gardens of the land. Every portion of the shore is inhabited by its peculiar species of these delicate algæ. At high-water mark we see the great black thongs of the bladder-wrack, and the pea-green laver; at low-water mark and in the tide-pools, we have the pink and roseate kinds, for these latter die, like so many fishes, if removed from the incessant contact of the water, and soon bleach into melancholy films. Ponds, rivers, even ditches, have their special vegetable inhabitants. Where the water is clear and still, there are water-lilies, anchored far from the land, and often with beautiful spires and campaniles of other plants rising among them, like a floral Venice. No timorous hand reaches these. As "faint heart never won fair lady," so may it be said of the water-lilies. To secure these, it is of no use to stand on the brink and sigh. Ingenuity and perseverance will, nevertheless, bring them to land, and then how lovely and pure a form! The white water-lily is closely allied, both in form and nature, to that mystic Lotus of the Nile, representatives of which, carved in stone, are still preserved upon the monuments of Egypt, where the plant was regarded as a sacred and natural hieroglyph, and where, doubtless, its purity and lustre conveyed their right and ample meaning.

The water-lilies never grow in foul water, and always

prefer that which is in steady though slow movement, loving especially the little bays along the edges, where they can spread their broad leaves upon the surface undisturbed, and expand their argent cups, brimming with golden stamens, to the light of the sun. Towards evening they close their petals in a kind of sleep, and during the period of their highest life, which is that of the preparation of the seed that is to renew the plant, they not only close, but sink below the surface of the stream. In many kinds the odor is rich and delicate, and some sorts yield eatable seeds. The Egyptian Lotus bore a rose-colored flower; but that does not interfere with the beautiful concordance of these plants with the ideas of truth and chastity — rather does it confirm the correspondence. Clear and moving water, broad and elegant leaves, pure white or rose-colored flowers, odor, modesty of life, and withdrawal in times of darkness — how beautifully all these characteristics of the water-lily and the lotus combine to show us what they signify in the language of nature!

What a contrast with the sea-weeds is found in trees! Here in the north all our trees are much branched, and, when full grown, form grand umbrageous sun-shades, to which we can retire for shelter when the summer heats fall fiercely upon our cheeks; their boughs in many cases decline elegantly towards the ground, so that we can reach their nuts and acorns; and in winter, when they have cast aside their foliage for awhile, we see a wonderful diversity in their styles of architecture; some are massive, and seem to belong to the heroic ages, as the oak and the chesnut; others, like the birch and the acacia, are graceful and delicate, **and** seem feminine **companions** of the manly ones. In the **tropics,** on the **other hand, there are not only branching trees such as those of the north,** though enormously greater in their **development, but trees** that are wholly devoid of branches, **rising like tall** pillars of wood, **perfectly erect,** and **to a** prodigious **height, with a** crown of immense leaves **upon the very summit. These are the** palm-trees, **the princes of the equatorial zone, as the** pine **and cedar trees are the princes of the temperate zones. In England we only see them in conservatories, as at Kew and Chatsworth.** They want much **more light and natural atmospheric warmth than are ever rendered to them in Britain, and thus form a peculiar and magnificent characteristic of the tropics, filling the traveller with admiration, and awakening all his sense of tropical grandeur of vegetation.**

> "Yet who in Indian bower hath stood,
> But thought on England's good green wood;
> And breathed a sigh, how oft in vain,
> To gaze upon her oaks again!"

In the extreme **north of Europe, and in the northern** parts of America, **there are forests** consisting **exclusively of pines and firs, and of such vast area that many days'** travel is required to traverse **them. They are evergreen; the** animals and birds **inhabiting them are very few; human** habitations **are scarcely known, except upon their** borders, where they **adjoin cultivated or** pasture land; and hence **they form at** once the **most monotonous of woods and the sublimest of solitudes.**

It is here, as during the darkness of night, in solitary places down by the sea, when we have wandered away from the sound of men and the view of lamps, that we feel the littleness of ourselves and the brevity of this temporal life. Everything around is grand, solemn, and perennial; we are driven inwards upon ourselves, and live for the time in that little secret chamber which we all have in the inmost of our hearts, into which only God and ourselves can enter, and where we meet face to face. Even our English woods, in their green depths and inexpressible seclusion, give much of this feeling when we enter them alone; and it is good to do so, and to receive their healthy and happy influences. Our English woods differ greatly from those silent pine-woods in the abundance of their living creatures, and equally so in the plenty of their flowers and ferns. Hence there is much to attract the eyes and thoughts; but, over and above all, there is the inexpressible feeling of the isolation, and the nearness of Him who made them all. It is well to visit these great solitudes, for no places more powerfully awaken us to the Divine appeal, "Have I been so long time with you, and yet hast thou not known me, Philip?"

Thus do we find in all countries of the world, upon land and in water, plants appropriate to their several stations, and every place being rendered cheerful and beautiful by their presence. What would have been the case had plants all required an equal amount of warmth and protection, or an equal amount of moisture? Many spots would have been barren, and the enjoyments of man have been reduced in proportion. But go where we will, we meet with new illustrations of the Divine Benevolence — the true idea of the omnipresence of God is that in every place we find the manifestations of His providence.

Disclosures of the Microscope.

MENTION has more than once been made in the preceding papers of the exquisite and marvellous spectacles presented through the medium of the microscope. We propose now to describe some of these in detail, since it is through the use of this miraculous instrument that we are enabled to view not merely the little things of nature, but the otherwise unknown. We delight in the consideration of how much our eyes behold —trees, animals, the sea, the sky, flowers, the unfathomable beauty of the human soul, as set forth in the various expression of the countenance, when the spirit lives in light and freedom ; we are apt to overlook the fact that our unassisted eyes do not introduce us to more than the half of the world in the midst of which we dwell ; thus that we delight in what is really no more than very partial knowledge. And if intelligent and loving interest in the obvious things of nature possess the power—as we are assured that it does by those who have tried—of giving length to human existence, by multiplying ideas, which constitute, after all, the only realities in life, how grand an *elixir vitæ* must be supplied by the delicate and unconsidered atoms that exist beyond the line to which our ordinary vision reaches. Possibly, were the eye of man so formed as for him to behold, without the aid of its lenses, the minute organisms that the microscope brings into view — possibly it might not then be able to pierce the infinite altitudes, read the story of the stars and the planets, and the immortal harmonies we call the heavens, and which are the pictures and preludes of the higher and original heavens to be entered some day. To me it seems a striking feature in the Divine Benevolence that the eye should be constructed as we find it — able, of its own independent power, to traverse millions of miles, and to rest upon the light of spheres so distant as Arcturus and Pleiades, "shedding sweet influence;" and at the same time, by virtue of the added power which the ingenuity of science bestows, that it should be able to penetrate as remotely in the other direction. For what space is in regard to the spheres that astronomy deals with, minuteness is in relation to those which pertain to the realm of the microscope. Were our eyes fitted to behold, ordinarily and familiarly, the infinite little, and were the infinitely-distant to be the privilege only of the philosopher with the telescope, it is probable that the whole current of human thought would be different, — unquestionably it would not be so noble, — certainly men would be less impressed with the awfulness and the grandeur of the universe. Seeing them only casually, and many men never seeing them at all, the stars would be a mere fable of science, instead of the princely inheritance of every human being. Therefore may we thank God that he gives us, unsought, so much glory, and yet permits to the same organ that commands the sweet lustre of the winter skies a corresponding power to interpret the invisible in the world of nature.

The range of the human eye may be judged of from a consideration which gives us at the same time a good idea of the scope of animal structure. Supposing that an individual of every known species were to take its stand between the two species that were respectively the next larger and the next smaller than itself, the smallest known animal being at one extremity of the line, and the largest standing at the other; and then supposing we were to ask which creature occupied the *middle* place, having as many degrees of size below it as above, and as many above it as below, that place would be found to be occupied by the common housefly. What a stupendous optical instrument must that be which, assisted with a few brass tubes and some disks of glass, shall discern a creature as much smaller than a fly as a fly is smaller than an elephant!

Perhaps the most strikingly beautiful of the microscopic things of nature are found among those minute and countless forms of vegetable life which ordinarily are termed mildews and blight. At nearly every period of the year, but principally in late summer and autumn, there is scarcely a plant of magnitude that does not afford an example. They are not necessarily pernicious; many species, without question, are injurious, causing quaint distortions, consuming the substance of the leaf or other portion of the plant they may be seated upon, and eating into it as rust eats into iron. Others, however, appear to be more of the nature of the mosses and lichens that so beautifully embroider and emboss the bark of the aged tree; that is to say, they are simply *epiphytes*, dwelling upon the plant without damaging it, and comparable to the birds that build their pretty cradles among the branches. When moderately magnified, these little vegetables present forms of the most exquisite symmetry, and are so amazingly varied that the nobler shapes of plants seem but fulfilments on a larger scale of designs primarily set forth in themselves. The realization of this fact by the mind, when we turn away from the charming spectacle that we may reflect awhile, is the highest reward that comes of the scrutiny. From the lowest nature upwards, every object and every phenomenon is a proem. Complete in itself, accomplishing a destiny, rounding off a period, giving the last touch of perfection to some profound and beautiful economy, every object in nature is at the same moment pre-significant of something to follow. Thus is it wise to dive into the world occupied by these pigmies; for while amid them we dwell with the earliest utterances, and going thence into the world of great things, the latter smile upon us as familiar faces. One of the prettiest of the pigmies is a species of the common blue mould called *Aspergillus*. The name refers to the resemblance it bears to the brush used in Roman Catholic religious services for scattering holy water, every plant consisting of a slender stalk, and at the summit a tuft of beaded filaments. Another, quite as elegant, but totally different, is found in profusion upon the leaves of the coltsfoot, which it ornaments underneath with yellow patches. Every patch, when magnified, becomes a crowd of fairy vases, the rims notched and thrown backwards like the petals of a flower! Botanists have discriminated many hundred species of this race of plants, and the number is daily on the increase. Not that new ones come into existence, but that careful observation quickens the eyes to see what was overlooked before, though passed by not only season after season, but day after day. As fresh air and early enjoyment of it are the best of cosmetics, so is natural history the best of eye-salves.

Transferring our attention to the Mosses, in addition to the prefigurement of flowers, we have that of the most stately and regal of trees. For the latter, the microscope is not needed. Every wood contains those incomparable miniatures of the oak and chesnut which botanists call *Hypnum dendroides*. Where the climate and soil are congenial, they give us *imperium in imperio*, one kingdom within another; the umbrageous patriarchs overhead supply nothing further in form and profile than is already expressed in their delicate arborescence. Very pleasing is it to the contemplative thus to find as a carpet for the feet, the same delineations that make life in the forest a delightful renewal of youth. Take their little flowers: no gem of the garden will excel them. In the Hypnum above referred to, and in all of its genus, the youngest state of the flowers presents nothing very remarkable, any more than do the buds of true flowers—always excepting the buds of the rose, which stand alone in presenting qualities as lovely as those of the fully-expanded blossom. When, however, a rather advanced condition has been reached, we seem, at first sight, to have the prototype of a daisy; a circlet of rays spreads from the margin of a round cup, which reminds us of the milk-white aureola of that pretty field-flower. These, however, so far from being petals, constitute an exquisite hygrometric lid of many pieces, protecting the entrance to the seed-capsule, which latter part the cup really consists of. Sometimes the rays are like gold; sometimes they are rose-color, with horizontal yellow bars; in some species they are forked, in others bent inwards; in none, however, except among the plants called *Phascum*, do they fail to appear under one form or another. The study of these unconsidered little productions is enough for any man's leisure, and in the pursuit of it he becomes a child over again; that is to say, he lives over again in the intense and inexpressible surprises and sensations of novelty that make up so large a portion of the heavenly era of early life. While it is good that in entering upon the study of philosophy we seek to do so with the meekness and humility of a little child, among the mosses, with a fair microscope in the hands, we are children once more, without knowing it, yea, whether we will or no. Whatever tends to foster and keep alive the emotions and susceptibilities of childhood, is precious beyond all measure; for though manhood gives exaltation to pleasures, and though pleasures of the highest dignity only become possible when youth has passed away, the keenest and most vivid relish still belongs to the childlike heart that is simple without being juvenile, and joyfully expectant without the aid of illusion.

Further, there is inconceivable richness and variety for the student who works with the microscope, in the aquatics which, when they dwell or are found in the country of the mermaids, we call "sea-weeds," but which, when inhabiting streams and fountains, are "fresh-water algæ." The green and downy mazes that float a little below the surface of the water in a still pond, consist of an infinite number of attenuated threads; these in turn are composed of an infinite number of hollow green beads, placed end to end, and firmly cemented together; and in the cavity of each bead — for every one of them is an independent cell — lies a drop of fluid with a floating island formed of substance more exquisite yet. The lovely pink sea-weeds that lie stranded upon the brown wet sand, uncovered by the retiring waves, differ from these only in the vastly larger number of their cells, and in the latter forming broad plates instead of being disposed in necklace-like strings. Both forms are, if possible, exceeded in beauty by a host of minute organisms, which consist of only a couple of cells. Such are the various species of *Micrasterias*. More wonderful yet is the *Volvox*, for in this is superadded to exquisite beauty the power of *movement*. Yet the volvox is a plant as truly as an oak-tree or a lily. We are accustomed to regard movement as one of the grand credentials of animal nature. True, in the waving of the trees when the wind creeps among their branches, and in the wave of light that runs over the cornfield, when gently stirred by the breeze, making it seem a vegetable sea — true, there is movement here, and in the sensitive-plant we seem to have absolute upon ourselves, and upon those about us, and **upon** Nature, with more marvel, and more love,—whatever does this, is essentially music. Thanks be to the Framer, that He has so framed human senses that they may receive it!

Animal-life, in its infinite variety of presentation; the beautiful stories that crystals can tell; and a thousand other particulars that lie in the great heart of Nature, but that come forth at the first call of the microscope, belong also to the romance of this **wonderful instrument.** Here, however, for the present, we must pause. It is well that between the acts there should be leisure for the voice of a minstrel.

> "These are Thy glorious works, Parent of good,
> Almighty, Thine this universal frame,
> Thus wondrous fair; Thyself how wondrous then!
> Unspeakable, **who** sit'st above these heavens,
> To us invisible **or dimly** seen
> In these Thy lowest **works**; yet these declare
> Thy goodness **beyond thought, and power divine.**"

www.ingramcontent.com/pod-product-compliance
Lightning Source LLC
Chambersburg PA
CBHW020310090426
42735CB00009B/1301